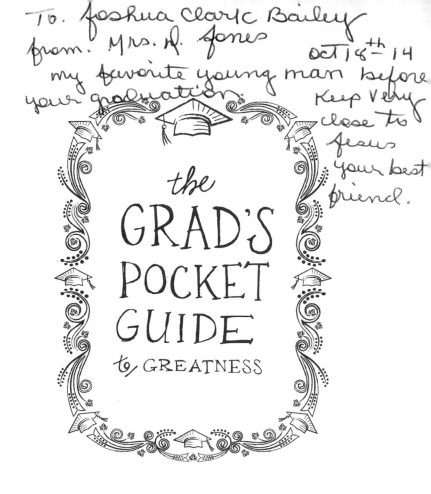

the GRAD'S POCKET GUIDE to GREATNESS

Compiled and Introduced by
JENNY YOUNGMAN

Abingdon Press
NASHVILLE

CONTENTS

INTRODUCTION

HERE YOU STAND AT A PIVOTAL MOMENT IN YOUR LIFE. YOU ARE GRADUATING. You have put in the time, done the hard work, sacrificed at times, and you are walking across that stage. Congratulations!

Now you look down the road at the next part of your journey and you have some options. Will you just get by? Will you float through your life? Or for the more exciting adventure, will you seek greatness? Will you seek excellence? Will you love and live well? Will you work hard, worship fully, and serve freely? From this place, you get to choose how you'll get from here to where you want to be. And you know what? Many, many wise people have gone before you. They have stood in your shoes and looked out into their future just as you are now.

Along the way, you may find yourself in need of some guidance or encouragement. This book is meant to be a traveling companion for your road ahead. Saints, sages, spiritual leaders, and others have paved the way and left some wisdom for those who would follow. Keep this book in your backpack or on your nightstand and scour its pages regularly for a pat on the back, an inspiration, a glimpse of hope, or a word of love and grace.

As you begin your road to greatness, remember what Jesus called the greatest commandment: to love God with all you've got and love others just the same. That is the starting point for you. Now go and Be Optimistic. Be Yourself. Be Wise. Be humble. Be Confident. Be forgiving. Be compassionate. Be creative. Be God's. Be Great!

> You must love the Lord your God with all your heart, with all your being, and with all your mind. This is the first and greatest commandment. And the second is like it: You must love your neighbor as you love yourself. All the Law and the Prophets depend on these two commands.
> —Matthew 22:37-40 (CEB)

CHAPTER I
BE OPTIMISTIC

WHO KNOWS WHAT TOMORROW WILL BRING? ONLY GOD. AND YOU KNOW WHAT? God promises that God's future for you is full of hope and peace. God's promises are completely trustworthy. You can look out at your future with full optimism, that no matter what comes your way, you belong to a God who has good plans in mind for you.

Surely, life will get you down. But don't let your failures make you cynical. Instead, count on God to show up in surprising and wonderful ways just when you think hope is lost!

I know the plans I have in mind for you, declares
the Lord; they are plans for peace, not disaster,
to give you a future filled with hope.
—Jeremiah 29:11 (CEB)

All life is an experiment.
The more experiments
you make, the better.

—*Journals of Ralph Waldo Emerson*

Sovereign Lord, I put my hope in you; I have
trusted in you since I was young. I have relied on
you all my life; you have protected me since the
day I was born. I will always praise you.
—Psalm 71:5-6 (GNT)

Be joyful in hope, patient in
affliction, faithful in prayer.
—Romans 12:12 (NIV)

That it will never come again
Is what makes life so sweet.
—Emily Dickinson, Poem 1741

Unrelenting disappointment
leaves you heartsick, but a sudden
good break can turn life around.
—Proverbs 13:12 *(THE MESSAGE)*

Life is a boundless privilege, and when you pay
for your ticket, and get into the car, you have no
guess what good company you will find there.
—Ralph Waldo Emerson, *The Conduct of Life*

Abraham was first named "father" and then
became a father because he dared to trust God
to do what only God could do: raise the dead to
life, with a word make something out of nothing.
When everything was hopeless, Abraham
believed anyway, deciding to live not on the basis
of what he saw he couldn't do but on what God
said he would do. And so he was made father of a
multitude of peoples. God himself said to him,
"You're going to have a big family, Abraham!"
—Romans 4:17-18 *(THE MESSAGE)*

Sustain me, according to your promise,
    and I will live;
  do not let my hopes be dashed.
—Psalm 119:116 (NIV)

The glory of God is a human being fully alive.

—Irenaeus, *Against Heresies*

Whenever anyone asks you to speak of your
hope, be ready to defend it.
—1 Peter 3:15 (CEB)

'Tis always morning somewhere.
—Henry Wadsworth Longfellow, "The Poet's
Tale, The Birds of Killingsworth"

"Hope" is the thing with feathers,
That perches in the soul,
And sings the tune without the words,
And never stops—at all.
—Emily Dickinson, "Hope"

Standing on the promises, I cannot fall,
Listening every moment to the Spirit's call,
Resting in my Savior as my all in all,
Standing on the promises of God.
—R. Kelso Carter, "Standing on the Promises"

BE NOT AFRAID

of life.

BELIEVE

that life is worth living,

****

and your belief
will
help create
THE FACT.

****

WILLIAM JAMES
The Will to Believe

CHAPTER 2
BE YOURSELF

SELF-DISCOVERY IS ONE OF
LIFE'S GREATEST JOURNEYS. From
the days of preschool to the halls of
middle school to the pledge days of
college and beyond we learn a little
more about who we are and how we are
wired every single day. As you step into your
skin and discover just who God made you to be,
remember that you are you and no one else can be.
You are one of a kind, and you have a one-of-a-
kind story to tell with your life. Be yourself—there
will never be another you!

For you created my inmost being; you knit me
    together in my mother's womb.
I praise you because I am fearfully and
    wonderfully made; your works are wonderful, I
    know that full well.
—Psalm 139: 13-14 (NIV)

**You are altogether beautiful,
my love; there is no flaw in you.
—Song of Solomon 4:7 (ESV)**

We are God's accomplishment, created in Christ
Jesus to do good things. God planned for these
good things to be the way that we live our lives.
—Ephesians 2:10 (CEB)

**Don't let anyone make fun of you, just because
you are young. Set an example for other
followers by what you say and do, as well as by
your love, faith, and purity.
—1 Timothy 4:12 (CEV)**

Are not two sparrows sold for a penny? And not
one of them will fall to the ground apart from your
Father. But even the hairs of your head are all
numbered. Fear not, therefore; you are of more
value than many sparrows.
—Matthew 10:29-31 (ESV)

But the Lord said to Samuel, "Have no regard for his appearance or stature, because I haven't selected him. God doesn't look at things like humans do. Humans see only what is visible to the eyes, but the Lord sees into the heart."
—1 Samuel 16:7 (CEB)

[Be who you are and say what you feel because] those who mind don't matter and those who matter don't mind.
—Barnard Baruch
Shake Well Before Using (Cerf)

To love oneself is the beginning of a life-long romance.
—Oscar Wilde, *Epigrams*

What I propose to do now is to try listening to my life as a whole, or at least to certain key moments of the first half of my life thus far, for whatever of meaning, or holiness of God, there may be in it to hear. My assumption is that the story of any one of us is in some measure the story of us all.
—Fredrick Buechner, *Listening to Your Life*

The whole secret of a successful life is to find out
what it is one's destiny to do, and then to do it.
—Henry Ford, "Success"

No one man, for any considerable period, can
wear one face to himself, and another to the
multitude, without finally getting bewildered as
to which may be the true.
—Nathaniel Hawthorne, *The Scarlet Letter*

The Lord detests people with crooked hearts, but
he delights in those with integrity.
—Proverbs 11:20 (NLT)

Once I asked my confessor for advice about my
vocation. I asked, "How can I know if God is
calling me and for what he is calling me?"
He answered, "You will know by your happiness.
If you are happy with the idea that God calls you
to serve him and your neighbor, this will be proof
of your vocation. Profound joy of the heart is like
a magnet that indicates the path of life."
—Mother Teresa, *My Life for the Poor*

Promise me you'll always remember: You're
braver than you believe, and stronger than you
seem, and smarter than you think.
—A. A. Milne, *Pooh's Grand Adventure*

CHAPTER 3
BE WISE

WISDOM, PRUDENCE,
DISCERNMENT—THESE ARE ALL
THINGS THAT ARE LEARNED WITH
EXPERIENCE. You are going to make
some great decisions. You are going to
make some terrible decisions. The great thing is
that with each decision, you will get a little wiser.
Wisdom is not something that you can master; you
can always gain more and grow wiser with each
step of life. The catch with wisdom is that it begins
with prayer— a step toward God. And God
promises to meet us with wisdom when we ask
God for it.

But anyone who needs wisdom should ask God,
whose very nature is to give to everyone without
a second thought, without keeping score.
Wisdom will certainly be given to those who ask.
—James 1:5 (CEB)

Apply your heart to instruction
and your ear to words of knowledge.
—Proverbs 23:12 (ESV)

By wisdom a house is built;
    by understanding it is established.
By knowledge rooms are filled
    with all precious and pleasant wealth.
A wise person is mightier
    than a strong one;
    a knowledgeable person
        than a powerful one.
You should make war with guidance;
    victory comes with many counselors.
Wisdom is beyond foolish people.
    They don't open their mouths
        in the gate.
—Proverbs 24:3-7 (CEB)

The least of the work of
learning is done in the classrooms.
—Thomas Merton, *Love and Living*

Wisdom resides
in an understanding heart,
but it's not known in fools.
—Proverbs 14:33 (CEB)

Wisdom begins with the fear of the LORD,
but fools despise wisdom
and instruction.
—Proverbs 1:7 (CEB)

Wherever
there is truth,
it is the Lord's.
—attributed to Justin Martyr

Do you want to be counted wise, to build a
reputation for wisdom? Here's what you do: Live
well, live wisely, live humbly. It's the way you live,
not the way you talk, that counts. Mean-spirited
ambition isn't wisdom. Boasting that you are wise
isn't wisdom. Twisting the truth to make
yourselves sound wise isn't wisdom. It's the
furthest thing from wisdom.
—James 3:13-16 *(THE MESSAGE)*

Take good counsel and accept correction—
that's the way to live wisely and well.
—Proverbs 19:20 *(THE MESSAGE)*

Every scripture is inspired by God and is useful
for teaching, for showing mistakes, for correcting,
and for training character, so that the person who
belongs to God can be equipped to do
everything that is good.
—2 Timothy 3:16-17 (CEB)

Education is that which remains, if one has
forgotten everything he learned in school.
—Albert Einstein, *Out of My Later Years*

God, grant me the serenity
to accept the things I cannot change,
the courage to change the things I can,
and the wisdom to know the difference.

Reinhold Niebuhr, sermon, 1943

Men and women who have lived wisely and well will shine brilliantly, like the cloudless, star-strewn night skies.

And those who put others

on the right path to life

will glow like stars

FOREVER.

Daniel 12:3 *(THE MESSAGE)*

It is the trained, living human soul, cultivated and strengthened by long study and thought, that breathes the real breath of life into boys and girls and makes them human, whether they be black or white, Greek, Russian, or American.
—W. E. B. DuBois, *The Negro Problem*

> Liberty without learning is always in peril and learning without liberty is always in vain.
> —John F. Kennedy, speech, Vanderbilt University, March 18, 1963

Anyone who listens to my teaching and follows it is wise, like a person who builds a house on solid rock. Though the rain comes in torrents and the floodwaters rise and the winds beat against that house, it won't collapse because it is built on bedrock. But anyone who hears my teaching and doesn't obey it is foolish, like a person who builds a house on sand. When the rains and floods come and the winds beat against that house, it will collapse with a mighty crash.
—Matthew 7:24-27 (NLT)

CHAPTER 4
BE HUMBLE

HAVE YOU EVER KNOWN ANYONE WHO WAS COMPLETELY FULL OF HIMSELF? He stares a little too long into the mirror. He walks in and expects people to take notice. He expects to be waited upon. He expects to be seen and heard? As you prepare to take the next steps in your journey, make a promise to yourself to never, under any circumstances, be that guy. Instead, listen to Jesus who teaches us to be humble, who was the ultimate example of humility himself. Take him at his word that those who humble themselves will indeed be lifted up.

*Pride makes us artificial
and humility makes us real.*
Attributed to Thomas Merton

For all those who exalt themselves will be
humbled, and those who humble themselves
will be exalted.
—Luke 14:11 (NIV)

Therefore, as God's chosen people,
holy and dearly loved, clothe
yourselves with compassion, kindness,
humility, gentleness and patience.
—Colossians 3:12 (NIV)

The stuck-up fall flat on their faces,
but down-to-earth people stand firm.
—Proverbs 11:2 *(THE MESSAGE)*

He has showed you, O man, what is good.
And what does the LORD require of you?
To act justly and to love mercy
and to walk humbly with your God.
—Micah 6:8 (NIV)

Pride comes before disaster,
 and arrogance before a fall.
—Proverbs 16:18 (CEB)

But the grace that God gives is even stronger.
As the scripture says, "God resists the proud,
but gives grace to the humble."
—James 4:6 (GNT)

You know more than you think you know, just as
you know less than you want to know.
—Oscar Wilde, *The Picture of Dorian Grey*

The reward of humility
and the fear of the LORD
is wealth, honor, and life.
—Proverbs 22:4 (CEB)

If the only prayer you said in your whole life was
"thank you" that would suffice.
—attributed to Meister Eckhart

> Humility is to make a right estimate of one's self.
> —Charles Spurgeon, sermon "Pride and Humility"

In the same way, I urge you who are younger:
accept the authority of the elders. And everyone,
clothe yourselves with humility toward each other.
God stands against the proud, but he gives favor
to the humble.
—1 Peter 5:5 (CEB)

> When I look up at your skies,
> at what your fingers made—
> the moon and the stars
> that you set firmly in place—
> what are human beings
> that you think about them;
> what are human beings
> that you pay attention to them?
> —Psalm 8:3-4 (CEB)

I claim to be a simple individual liable to err like
any other fellow mortal. I own, however, that I
have humility enough to confess my errors and to
retrace my steps.
—attributed to Mohandas Gandhi

My life is not for itself and not for a spectacle. I
much prefer that it should be of a lower strain, so
it be genuine and equal, than that it should be
glittering and unsteady.
—Ralph Waldo Emerson, *Self-Reliance*

> **Nothing is more deceitful than the appearance
> of humility. It is often only carelessness of
> opinion, and sometimes an indirect boast.**
> **—Jane Austen, *Pride and Prejudice***

Because of the privilege and authority God has
given me, I give each of you this warning: Don't
think you are better than you really are. Be honest
in your evaluation of yourselves, measuring
yourselves by the faith God has given us.
—Romans 13:3 (NLT)

Only a life lived for others
is the life worthwhile.

—Albert Einstein
New York Times, June 20, 1932

CHAPTER 5
BE CONFIDENT

YOU MIGHT THINK THAT HUMILITY AND CONFIDENCE DON'T GO TOGETHER. To be sure, you can overdo confidence and become egotistical just like you can overdo humility and become pitiful. You will need both to be great in this life. You will need an unyielding belief in your ability to accomplish your dreams and in God's promise to be faithful to complete God's work in you. You will also need that humility to remember where our abilities and dreams came from.

I pray that God, the source of hope, will fill you
completely with joy and peace because you trust
in him. Then you will overflow with confident hope
through the power of the Holy Spirit.
—Romans 15:13 (NLT)

The LORD will be your confidence;
he will guard your feet
from being snared.
—Proverbs 3:26 (CEB)

Start by doing what is necessary,
then what is possible, and suddenly
you are doing the impossible.
—Saint Francis of Assisi

The LORD is my light and my salvation;
whom shall I fear?
The LORD is the stronghold of my life;
of whom shall I be afraid?
When evildoers assail me
to eat up my flesh,
my adversaries and foes,
it is they who stumble and fall.
Though an army encamp against me,
my heart shall not fear;
though war arise against me,
yet I will be confident.
—Psalm 27:1-3

You gain STRENGTH, COURAGE, and CONFIDENCE by every experience in which you really stop to look fear in the face. You are able to say to yourself, "I have lived through this horror. I can take the next thing that comes along." . . .

You must do the thing you think you cannot do.

—Eleanor Roosevelt, *You Learn by Living*

I pray that God, the source of hope, will fill you
completely with joy and peace because you trust
in him. Then you will overflow with confident
hope through the power of the Holy Spirit.
—Romans 15:13 (NLT)

Some trust in chariots and some in horses,
but we trust in the name of the LORD our God.
—Psalm 20:7 (ESV)

No one can make you feel inferior
without your consent.
—attributed to Eleanor Roosevelt

Don't be afraid, for I am with you.
Don't be discouraged, for I am your God.
I will strengthen you and help you.
I will hold you up with my victorious right hand.
—Isaiah 41:10 (NLT)

Once faced and settled there really wasn't any
good reason to refer to [the "Friendship" flight] again.
—Amelia Earhart, *20 Hours: 40 Minutes—
Our Flight in the* Friendship

Whatever you say, say it with conviction.
—attributed to Mark Twain

Avoiding danger is no safer in the
long run than outright exposure.
The fearful are caught as often as the bold.
—Helen Keller, Let Us Have Faith

**If one advances confidently in the direction of
his dreams, and endeavors to live the life which
he has imagined, he will meet with a success
unexpected in common hours.
—Henry David Thoreau, *Walden***

Commit your work to the Lord, and your plans
will succeed.
—Proverbs 16:3 (CEB)

Make the most
of yourself, for that is
all there is of you.

attributed to
Ralph Waldo Emerson

CHAPTER 6
BE FORGIVING

ANGER, GRUDGES,
CONFLICT, AND DISCORD WILL BE WAITING IN THE WINGS to steal your joy and bring you bitterness and fatigue. But you can bob and weave and fight against it. How? Forgive. When you forgive, you let go of the anger and keep that bitter root from growing within you. It can be one of your greatest defense moves.

I heard a great sermon once saying that forgiveness is more about how it changes the forgiver than the one being forgiven. The preacher said that it doesn't even matter if the person accepts the forgiveness. The act of forgiveness itself is the move that saves you from growing bitter.

Jesus was matter-of-fact: "Embrace this God-life. Really embrace it, and nothing will be too much for you. This mountain, for instance: Just say, 'Go jump in the lake'—no shuffling or shilly-shallying—and it's as good as done. That's why I urge you to pray for absolutely everything, ranging from small to large. Include everything as you embrace this God-life, and you'll get God's everything. And when you assume the posture of prayer, remember that it's not all asking. If you have anything against someone, forgive—only then will your heavenly Father be inclined to also wipe your slate clean of sins."
—Mark 11:22-25 *(THE MESSAGE)*

The weak can never forgive. Forgiveness is the attribute of the strong.

—Mohandas Gandhi
Young India

People are often unreasonable and self-centered.
Forgive them anyway.
If you are kind, people may accuse you
of ulterior motives. Be kind anyway.
If you are honest, people may cheat you.
Be honest anyway.
If you find happiness, people may be jealous.
Be happy anyway.
The good you do today may be forgotten
tomorrow. Do good anyway.
Give the world the best you have and it may
never be enough. Give your best anyway.
For you see, in the end, it is between you and
God. It was never between you and them anyway.
—attributed to Mother Teresa

> Forgiveness is an act of the will,
> and the will can function regardless
> of the temperature of the heart.
> —Corrie ten Boom

All have sinned and fall short of God's glory.
—Romans 3:23 (CEB)

> But if you don't forgive others, neither will your
> Father forgive your sins.
> —Matthew 6:15 (CEB)

Forgiveness is the fragrance the violet sheds
on the heel that has crushed it.
—attributed to Mark Twain

**To be a Christian means to forgive the
inexcusable because God has forgiven the
inexcusable in you.**
—C. S. Lewis

But when you are praying, first forgive anyone
you are holding a grudge against, so that your
Father in heaven will forgive your sins, too.
—Mark 11:25 (NLT)

The weak can never forgive.
Forgiveness is the attribute of the strong.
—Mohandas Gandhi, *Young India*

Always forgive your enemies;
nothing annoys them so much.
—attributed to Oscar Wilde

Forgive us for the ways we have wronged you,
just as we also forgive
those who have wronged us.
—Matthew 6:12 (CEB)

Then Peter said to Jesus, "Lord,

how many times should I forgive my

brother or sister who sins against

me? Should I **FORGIVE** as many as

seven times?" Jesus said, "Not just

seven times, but rather as many as

SEVENTY-SEVEN TIMES."

—*Matthew 18:21-22 (CEB)*

Make this your common practice: Confess your
sins to each other and pray for each other so that
you can live together whole and healed. The
prayer of a person living right with God is
something powerful to be reckoned with. Elijah,
for instance, human just like us, prayed hard that
it wouldn't rain, and it didn't—not a drop for three
and a half years. Then he prayed that it would
rain, and it did. The showers came and everything
started growing again.
—James 5:16-18 *(THE MESSAGE)*

To err is human,
to forgive, divine.
—Alexander Pope,
An Essay on Criticism

CHAPTER 7
BE COMPASSIONATE

PART OF THE GIFT YOU CAN GIVE THE WORLD IS TO LIVE COMPASSIONATELY—to extend grace, to give generously, to see the invisible ones in our society, to offer hope and help whenever you can. As we grow up into our walk with Christ, we begin to put on compassion like our clothing. We wear it, and it becomes part of our identity, an expression of what is important to us.

Therefore, as God's choice, holy and loved, put
on compassion, kindness, humility, gentleness,
and patience.
—Colossians 3:12 (CEB)

Be happy with those who are happy, and cry with
those who are crying.
—Romans 12:15 (CEB)

Those who are gracious to the poor
lend to the LORD,
and the Lord will fully repay them.
—Proverbs 19:17 (CEB)

The way God designed our bodies is a model for
understanding our lives together as a church:
every part dependent on every other part, the
parts we mention and the parts we don't, the
parts we see and the parts we don't. If one part
hurts, every other part is involved in the hurt,
and in the healing. If one part flourishes, every
other part enters into the exuberance.
—1 Corinthians 12:25-26 *(THE MESSAGE)*

No act of kindness, no matter
how small, is ever wasted.
—attributed to Aesop

The life of a man consists not in seeing visions,
and in dreaming dreams, but in active charity
and willing service.
—Henry Wadsworth Longfellow,
Kavanagh, A Tale

Summing up: Be agreeable, be sympathetic, be
loving, be compassionate, be humble. That goes
for all of you, no exceptions. No retaliation. No
sharp-tongued sarcasm. Instead, bless—that's
your job, to bless. You'll be a blessing and also get
a blessing.
Whoever wants to embrace life
    and see the day fill up with good,
Here's what you do:
    Say nothing evil or hurtful;
Snub evil and cultivate good;
    run after peace for all you're worth.
God looks on all this with approval,
    listening and responding well to what he's
        asked;
But he turns his back
    on those who do evil things.
—1 Peter 3:8-12 *(THE MESSAGE)*

Generosity is the flower of justice.
—Nathaniel Hawthorne, *Passages from the
American Notebooks*

A Samaritan traveling the road came on him. When he saw the man's condition, his heart went out to him. He gave him first aid, disinfecting and bandaging his wounds. Then he lifted him onto his donkey, led him to an inn, and made him comfortable. In the morning he took out two silver coins and gave them to the innkeeper, saying, 'Take good care of him. If it costs any more, put it on my bill—I'll pay you on my way back.'

"What do you think? Which of the three became a neighbor to the man attacked by robbers?"

"The one who treated him kindly," the religion scholar responded.

Jesus said, "Go and do the same."

—Luke 10:33-35 *(THE MESSAGE)*

But the LORD says,
"Because the poor are oppressed,
because of the groans of the needy,
I'm now standing up.
I will provide the help
they are gasping for."
—Psalm 12:5 (CEB)

Be kind,

for everyone you meet is fighting a harder battle.

—attributed to Ian McLaren
(a.k.a. John Watson)
occasionally attributed to Plato

The great miracle and mystery of God is that he calls me and you to be a part of what he is doing in history. He could, of course, with no help from us proclaim the gospel of Jesus Christ with lifeless stones, feed the entire world with five loaves and two fish, heal the sick with the hem of his garment, and release all the oppressed with his angels. Instead, God has chosen us— missionaries, agricultural engineers, doctors, lawyers, lawmakers, diplomats, and all those who support, encourage and pray for them—to be his hands in doing those things in the world that are important to him.

—Gary Haugen, *Good News About Injustice*

Compassion:

that sometimes fatal capacity for feeling
what it is like to live inside another's skin
and for knowing that there can never
really be peace and joy for any until
there is peace and joy finally for all.
—Fredrick Buechner,
The Alphabet of Grace

CHAPTER 8
BE CREATIVE

WE ARE MADE BY A CREATOR GOD WHO HAS GIFTED EACH OF US WITH TALENTS, ABILITIES, INCLINATIONS, IDEAS, DREAMS, AND HOPES. God even asks us to put our hands in to God's creative work and add our thumbprint to the great mural of Creation. That doesn't mean we're all artists or that we all need a craft room. It does mean that we get to figure out what it means for us to be creative using the gifts we've been given. How can using your gifts proclaim the glory of God to all the world?

Heaven is declaring God's glory;
    the sky is proclaiming his handiwork.
One day gushes the news to the next,
    and one night informs another
        what needs to be known.
Of course, there's no speech, no words—
    their voices can't be heard—
but their sound extends
    throughout the world;
    their words reach the ends
        of the earth.
—Psalm 19:1-4 (CEB)

Perhaps God is strong enough to exult in
monotony. It is possible that God says every
morning, "Do it again" to the sun; and every
evening, "Do it again" to the moon. It may not be
automatic necessity that makes all daisies alike;
it may be that God makes every daisy
separately, but has never got tired of making
them. It may be that He has the eternal appetite
of infancy; for we have sinned and grown old,
and our Father is younger than we. The
repetition in Nature may not be a mere
recurrence; it may be a theatrical encore.
—G. K. Chesterton, *Orthodoxy*

Whatever you do, do it from the heart for the
Lord and not for people.
—Colossians 3:23 (CEB)

> **Think left and think right and think low and think
> high. Oh, the thinks you can think up
> if only you try!**
> **—Dr. Seuss, *Oh, the Thinks You Can Think***

Then Moses said to the Israelites: "Look, the Lord
has chosen Bezalel, Uri's son and Hur's grandson
from the tribe of Judah. The Lord has filled him
with the divine spirit that will give him skill, ability,
and knowledge for every kind of work. He will be
able to create designs, do metalwork in gold,
silver, and copper, cut stones for setting, carve
wood, do every kind of creative work, and have
the ability to teach others. Both he and Oholiab,
Ahisamach's son from the tribe of Dan, have been
given the skill to do every kind of work done by a
gem cutter or a designer or a needleworker in
blue, purple, and deep red yarns and in fine linen
or a weaver or anyone else doing work or
creating designs."
—Exodus 35:30-35 (CEB)

We will see God reaching out to us in every wind that blows, every sunrise and sunset, every cloud in the sky, every flower that blooms, and every leaf that fades, if we will only use our starved imagination to visualize it.

—Oswald Chambers, *My Utmost for His Highest*

God can do anything, you know—far more than you could ever imagine or guess or request in your wildest dreams! He does it not by pushing us around but by working within us, his Spirit deeply and gently within us.
—Ephesians 3:20 *(THE MESSAGE)*

The kingdom of heaven is like a man who was leaving on a trip. He called his servants and handed his possessions over to them. To one he gave five valuable coins, and to another he gave two, and to another he gave one. He gave to each servant according to that servant's ability. Then he left on his journey. After the man left, the servant who had five valuable coins took them and went to work doing business with them. He gained five more.
—Matthew 25:14-16 (CEB)

Our duty, as men and women, is to proceed as if limits to our ability did not exist. We are collaborators in creation.
—attributed to Pierre Teilhard de Chardin

The place God calls you to is the place where your deep gladness and the worlds' deep hunger meet.
—Fredrick Buechner, *Listening to Your Life*

Hallelujah!
Praise God in his holy house of worship,
    praise him under the open skies;
Praise him for his acts of power,
    praise him for his magnificent greatness;
Praise with a blast on the trumpet,
    praise by strumming soft strings;
Praise him with castanets and dance,
    praise him with banjo and flute;
Praise him with cymbals and a big bass drum,
    praise him with fiddles and mandolin.
Let every living, breathing creature praise God!
    Hallelujah!
—Psalm 150:1-6 *(THE MESSAGE)*

Since love grows within you, so beauty grows. For love is the beauty of the soul.

—Augustine of Hippo

CHAPTER 9
BE GOD'S

WHEREVER YOU GO AND WHATEVER YOU DO, REMEMBER THAT YOU BELONG TO GOD.

God has called you by name. You are God's, and God is yours.

But now, GOD's Message,
    the God who made you in the first place, Jacob,
    the One who got you started, Israel:
"Don't be afraid, I've redeemed you.
    I've called your name. You're mine.
When you're in over your head, I'll be there with you.
    When you're in rough waters, you will not go down.
When you're between a rock and a hard place,
    it won't be a dead end—
Because I am GOD, your personal God,
    The Holy of Israel, your Savior.
I paid a huge price for you:
    all of Egypt, with rich Cush and Seba thrown in!
That's how much you mean to me!
    That's how much I love you!
I'd sell off the whole world to get you back,
    trade the creation just for you."
—Isaiah 43:1-4 (*THE MESSAGE*)

The Lord is my shepherd,

I have all that I need.

—Psalm 23:1 (NLT)

> I look up to the mountains—
> does my help come from there?
> My help comes from the LORD
> who made heaven and earth!
> —Psalm 121:1-2 (NLT)

But I trust in your unfailing love.
 I will rejoice because you have rescued me.
I will sing to the LORD
 because he is good to me.
—Psalm 13:5-6 (NLT)

> Until I am essentially united with God, I can
> never have full rest or real happiness.
> —attributed to Julian of Norwich

God so loved the world that he gave his only Son,
so that everyone who believes in him won't perish
but will have eternal life.
—John 3:16 (CEB)

> Imitate God, therefore, in everything you do,
> because you are his dear children. Live a life
> filled with love, following the example of Christ.
> —Ephesians 5:1 (NLT)

See what kind of love the Father has given to us in
that we should be called God's children, and that
is what we are!
—1 John 3:1 (CEB)

> My dear children, you come from God and
> belong to God. You have already won a big
> victory over those false teachers, for the Spirit in
> you is far stronger than anything in the world. . . .
> But we come from God and belong to God.
> —1 John 4:4-5 *(THE MESSAGE)*

As the deer longs for flowing streams,
 so my soul longs for you, O God.
—Psalm 42:1 (NRSV)

> I've told you these things for a purpose: that my
> joy might be your joy, and your joy wholly
> mature. This is my command: Love one another
> the way I loved you. This is the very best way to
> love. Put your life on the line for your friends.
> You are my friends when you do the things I
> command you. I'm no longer calling you
> servants because servants don't understand
> what their master is thinking and planning. No,
> I've named you friends because I've let you in on
> everything I've heard from the Father.
> —John 15:11-15 *(THE MESSAGE)*

Everlasting God,
In whom we live and move and have our being:
You have made us for yourself,
So that our hearts are restless
Until they rest in you.
—Augustine of Hippo, *Confessions*

You didn't choose me, remember; I chose you,
and put you in the world to bear fruit, fruit that
won't spoil.
—John 15:16 *(THE MESSAGE)*

Like sheep we get hungry for more than just
food. We get thirsty for more than just drink.
Our souls get hungry and thirsty; in fact it is
often that sense of inner emptiness that makes
us know we have souls in the first place. There is
nothing that the world has to give us, there is
nothing that we have to give to each other even,
that ever quite fills them.
—Fredrick Buechner, *Listening to Your Life*

I love those who love me;
those who seek me will find me.
—Proverbs 8:17 (CEB)

CHAPTER 10
BE GREAT

GREATNESS IS MEASURED NOT BY YOUR BANK ACCOUNT OR LETTERS AFTER YOUR NAME. It is not measured by the number of acquaintances or awards you acquire. Greatness is measured by the attitude of your heart, the generosity of your spirit, and the intention of your deeds. You can be great wherever you go and whatever you do when you commit your way to God and work as if working for the Lord. Congratulations on getting this far and blessings upon you as you walk the road to greatness.

For I can do everything through Christ
who gives me strength.
—Philippians 4:13 (NLT)

Don't copy the behavior and customs of this
world, but let God transform you into a new
person by changing the way you think. Then you
will learn to know God's will for you, which is
good and pleasing and perfect.
—Romans 12:2 (NLT)

The essence of greatness is
the perception that virtue is enough.
—Ralph Waldo Emerson, *Essays*

People plan their path,
but the LORD secures their steps.
—Proverbs 16:9 (CEB)

I don't mean to say that I have already achieved
these things or that I have already reached
perfection. But I press on to possess that
perfection for which Christ Jesus
first possessed me.
—Philippians 3:12 (NLT)

Always be joyful. Never stop praying.
—1 Thessalonians 5:16-17 (NLT)

If you try to hang on to your life, you will lose it.
But if you give up your life for my sake and for the
sake of the Good News, you will save it.
—Mark 8:35 (NLT)

It is a grand mistake to think of being great
without goodness; and I pronounce it as certain
there was never yet a truly great man that was
not at the same time truly virtuous.
—Benjamin Franklin, "The Busy-Body Papers"

But my life is worth nothing to me unless I use it
for finishing the work assigned me by the Lord
Jesus—the work of telling others the Good News
about the wonderful grace of God.
—Acts 20:24 (NLT)

America is too great for small dreams.
—Ronald Reagan, speech to Congress

Be not afraid of greatness: some are born great,
some achieve greatness, and some have
greatness thrust upon 'em.
—William Shakespeare, *Twelfth Night*

Have a heart that never hardens, a temper that
never tires, and a touch that never hurts.
—Charles Dickens, *Our Mutual Friend*

**Success is peace of mind, which is a direct result
of self-satisfaction in knowing you made the
effort to do your best to become the best that
you are capable of becoming.**
—John Wooden

Having, First, gained all you can, and, Secondly,
saved all you can, Then give all you can.
—John Wesley, Sermon 50, "The Use of Money"

**Christ with me, Christ before me, Christ behind
me, Christ in me, Christ beneath me, Christ
above me, Christ on my right, Christ on my left,
Christ when I lie down, Christ when I sit down,
Christ when I arise, Christ in the heart of every
man who thinks of me, Christ in the mouth of
every one who speaks of me, Christ in every eye
that sees me, Christ in every ear that hears me.**
—Lorica of Saint Patrick

Listen to your life. See it for the fathomless
mystery that it is. In the boredom and pain of it no
less in the excitement and gladness: touch, taste,
smell your way to the holy and hidden heart of it
because in the last analysis all moments are key
moments, and life itself is grace.
—Fredrick Buechner, *Listening to Your Life*

The price
of greatness
is
responsibility.

—Winston Churchill, "The Price of Greatness"

GUIDES TO GREATNESS

Aesop
Augustine of Hippo
Jane Austen
Barnard Baruch
Frederick Buechner
R. Kelso Carter
Oswald Chambers
G. K. Chesterton
Winston Churchill
Charles Dickens
Emily Dickinson
Pierre Teilhard de Chardin
Dr. Seuss
W. E. B. DuBois
Amelia Earhart
Meister Eckhart
Albert Einstein
Ralph Waldo Emerson
Henry Ford
Saint Francis
Benjamin Franklin
Mohandas Gandhi
Gary Haugen
Nathaniel Hawthorne
Irenaeus

William James
Mother Teresa
Julian of Norwich
Helen Keller
John F. Kennedy
C. S. Lewis
Henry Wadsworth Longfellow
Justin Martyr
Ian McLaren
Thomas Merton
A. A. Milne
Reinhold Niebuhr
Saint Patrick
Alexander Pope
Ronald Reagan
Eleanor Roosevelt
William Shakespeare
Charles Spurgeon
Corrie ten Boom
Henry David Thoreau
Mark Twain
John Wesley
Oscar Wilde
John Wooden